What Is Real?
George E. Johnson Jr.

Copyright © 2025 by George E. Johnson Jr.

All rights reserved.

No portion of this book may be reproduced in any form without written permission from the publisher or author, except as permitted by U.S. copyright law.

Contents

Forward I	1
Forward II	2
Introduction	3
What Is Real?	5
Background	6
Confessions	8
One Life	10
Saints	11
Our Source	12
The Rebirth of My Soul	13
The Vine	14
Reap What You Sow!	16
It's All So Clear	18
His Hands	20
Rules of the Game	21
Overcoming	23
You Are Not Alone!	25
Believer's Peace	26
That's L.I.T.!	28
The Highest Court	29
Tap In	31

Forgive Me	33
TRINITY	35
Precious Stone	36
Heaven Cries	38
Well Done!	40
Gratitude	41

Forward I

I've known George for a little while now, and I had the prestigious pleasure of performing the most sacred of honors. I was allowed to join him and his bride in a lifelong holy union. George is the definition of a gentle giant. His domineering frame is perfectly balanced with the juxtaposition of the eloquence of his words in poetry. He and his bride are true followers of Christ, and it truly shows in this phenomenal collection. This book is a perfect mix of scripture, wisdom, knowledge, and reflection. You WILL find yourself, your emotions, your thoughts, and feelings in these words and pages somewhere. You will find yourself relating to mentalities and experiences expressed here. Feel free to be vulnerable and explore your own feelings as you explore the pages of this work. I promise you will not be disappointed. Get ready.

Dr. Dewayne T. Washington
Senior Pastor - The Love Church
Owner – Facetime Studios
Co-Owner – Ebonyopoly
Published Author

Forward II

George Johnson has proven to be, through his musings, one of the most insightful, sensitive yet strong poets that we are blessed to have amongst us.

George has the ability to take complex thoughts and ideas that have multiple nuances and reduce them to palatable, meaningful, and relatable experiences. As with all expressions of art, it is designed to move the senses. Interacting with the poetry of George Johnson will move you through time and space in a way that will awaken your deepest innermost thoughts, conveying the reader to vistas unseen before. For such a time as this, George's writings are on the scene, and I believe many will be enlightened for years to come.

Joseph R. Fields
Founding/Sr. Pastor
New Beginnings Church

Introduction

Thank you for taking the time to consider this book as your next reading venture. I am truly honored and grateful to have the opportunity to show you, through poetry, that we are more than conquerors. In the stillness of life's trials, the melody of hope resonates through words that call us back to the Gospel's grace, love, and truth. I have been writing poetry for over twenty years and have had my poems published in the United States and the United Kingdom. Over the years, my style has evolved, and I have written poems exploring various aspects of culture, love, and life. I have finally completed a collection that I hope you all will love. This collection of gospel poetry is not just a reflection of the sacred but a journey of the soul in search of divine understanding and connection, focusing on faith, redemption, and hope. Each poem is a prayer, a song, a whisper of faith in the face of doubt, and a testament to the transformative power of God's love. I think it will propel us all into a world of joy. This collection will create a new genre called Gospel Poetry. While reading these selections, you will experience pain, long-suffering, joy, and triumph.

This book is a battle cry, a call to arms, for all Christians, whether you are aware of your spiritual gifts or not. It is also a book of gratitude and dedication to those who have helped me along the way, to let them know that their labor was not in vain. It is a window into my life and how I overcame many obstacles with faith. My desire to write this book has been a dream for over twenty years, during which I have experienced some struggles and triumphs.

This book will take you on a voyage, with each poem creating an image in your mind that will show you that redemption is real and that there is power in faith. Through these verses, I invite you to explore the depth of His grace, the strength of His mercy, and the unshakable foundation of His Word. In the pages ahead, you'll encounter the richness of scripture brought to life in rhythm and rhyme, revealing not just the beauty of the Gospel but its relevance to our everyday struggles, joys, and victories. I want to share with you how my faith has sustained me and guided me through overcoming some of my toughest challenges. I encourage you to gird your waist with truth, put on the breastplate of righteousness, shod your feet with the gospel of peace, take the shield of faith, the helmet of salvation, and the sword of the Spirit. I am honored to fight beside those who have been lost, forgotten, and wounded. May these words serve as a reminder of the unending love that surrounds us, guiding us through every season, and may they inspire you to walk in the light of His truth with renewed hope and unwavering faith. Welcome to a journey through Gospel poetry, where the Word meets the heart and the soul finds its true home.

What Is Real?

Real is the way...
that He loves me when I fall to my knees
And beg Him, "Father, forgive me, please!"
I sin against Him in many ways and many days,
But His love keeps saving me from the grave!

Real is the way...
that He gave His Son so that I may have eternal life,
Yet in this world, I know the difference between wrong and right.
The blood that He bled on Calvary is something that I will never feel.
But as time passes on, I realize that what He did was Real!

Real is the way...
that He saved my soul from drowning in the depths of Sin's Sea.
He heard my cry for help, my desperate plea.
When I was lost, and my friends were nowhere to be found,
He carried me on His back to make sure my feet were on solid ground!

Real is the way...
He tucks me in each night and wakes me up every day,
Making me humble as I get on my knees to pray.
God, we have a relationship stronger than Jonathan and David,
an unbreakable seal.
Because Lord, I give my soul to You!
Now, that's REAL!

Background

I was blessed to have two God-fearing parents in the home who were passionate about raising well-rounded children. They supported our endeavors and disciplined us with love. My father is a man of integrity who taught me the value of a strong work ethic, personal accountability, and a deep sense of responsibility. My mother's father was a pastor for over twenty years, so my mother has a deep belief in God and a strong faith. She taught me the importance of showing compassion, offering forgiveness, and having a belief in God.

I have two wonderful sisters. My oldest sister graduated as a valedictorian of our high school and earned both an undergraduate degree in Chemical Engineering and a Master of Business Administration. I have a twin sister who holds a Bachelor of Arts in Psychology, a Bachelor of Science in Communication Disorders, and a Master's degree in Deaf Studies/Deaf Education. She is currently employed as a Special Education Chairperson. My sisters encouraged, motivated, and inspired me to improve. I always looked up to them and sought out their wisdom and guidance. Then there was me, the only boy in our family. When I compared my accomplishments to those of my family, I did not feel like I measured up. I felt like there was something different about me. As the only black boys in our neighborhood, I was keenly aware that very few students in my school looked like me. Being a minority throughout my early education heightened the pressure of being different, which was not a reality shared by the rest of my family.

I lived under a different kind of pressure. As a young man with many unanswered questions about my people, I found some answers in the music of my culture. Music became my solace and a doorway to a world beyond the one I was raised in. It created a bridge that connected me to others like me, and I no longer felt so alone. I enjoyed the lyrics, the soulful rhythms, and the metaphors that added emotional depth to the music. Like music, I wanted to harness my creativity to bring something unique into this world. Music guided me on the path of poetry, deepened my connection to my culture, and helped me understand some of my history. It was in those years that I began to be lured to the serene songs of a carnal world. However, I recognized that music also stirred a unique creativity in me, and I wanted to bring this into the world. Ultimately, God used music to lead me to a path of poetry.

As an adolescent, I was shielded from certain aspects of the world, such as images of false gods and materialism. Knowing what I know now, I understand why. I was a young man with little understanding of how to interpret society, and I was somewhat easily influenced to give in to certain temptations. My college years served as a training ground for manhood, and the lessons I learned will stay with me for the rest of my life. I guess you could say, 'I was green.' I was unprepared for the social freedoms of college. I encountered a new environment filled with partying, drinking, fornication, and various related activities. I wanted to fit in and prove to my peers that I was cool and ready for any challenge; I wanted to demonstrate to my family that I could earn my degree and focus on my education; and I wanted to show myself that I was not just a waste of air. My life felt like a circus, a full-time juggling act between my righteous upbringing and the seductions of a life I aimed to master. These experiences would have a deep impact on my life for years to come. I was drawn into this lifestyle because I craved popularity and wanted to be part of the social phenomenon of college.

During those years, my flesh was winning the battle of my soul, and I allowed the temptations of this world to seduce me. My education was just something I did to buy myself time until I figured out what I wanted to do, but now that I look back, I am truly honored and grateful to have obtained my degree. Through it all, I continued writing, never recognizing this gift as an opportunity to change and possibly save lives. It is a chance to connect and relate to my culture and Believers on a deeper, more meaningful level.

After college, in the winter of 2000, I found myself completely lost and confused. Even though I had a college degree, I was unprepared for the real world. I did not take advantage of the opportunities to become the person, leader, and man I should have been. Foolishly, I believed I could overcome any obstacle, but in 2002, I found myself sleeping in my 1998 Nissan Sentra or wherever I could lay my head. No one thought that, due to my family and background, I would end up in that situation. I listened to the wrong people, took poor advice, and hoped for immediate success. I was there because of the decisions I had made in my life, and no one else was to blame. My life was going from bad to worse, and I asked myself, "Was this world worth dying for?", but that was not the right question. I should have asked myself, "Is Jesus worth living for?". Once I realized my life was not aligned with what I believed and moved past my me-mentality, I submitted to Jesus Christ, my Lord and Savior, the highest power.

Confessions

As I commune with you,
And you commune with me.
Let's put it all on the table
For the world to see.

There's a beast in me,
And I can't let go
He's been released and freed
And now you know!

He seduced my flesh
And he took control.
This was only a test,
It hypnotized my soul.

I was dazed and confused
By the grip of temptation.
And he was amused
Because of my damnation.

I was a slave to lust,
And that was my Queen.
She was hard to trust.
But she fulfilled my dream.

Greed, pride, and desire
They're all the same!
I dove into this fire,
I'm the one to blame.

I had to confess and repent
So, I could be redeemed.
This is not what God meant!
And it's not what it seems.

Satan took advantage of me,
I was just a beginner.
Unfortunately,
These are the Confessions of a Sinner.

One Life

All I have is one life,
To purify my polluted flesh.
One life to remove these demons from my chest.
Because on the limbs of my soul, there lies a nest
Where Satan used to rest,
And conceive demons to test
A soul that he didn't know was blessed.

All I need is one life,
To give You what's inside of me.
One life to prove, to You, how desperately-
The depths of my soul call for Thee.
And when they see
How Your love is impacting me,
Your children of this world
Will be set free.

You're all I have,
And for You, I will fight!
You are My Lord, and I am Your Knight.
When I cannot see, You are my light,
Guiding me with all of Your might.
Consider me a soldier, at no price.
This is our war,
So, I give to You "One Life."

Saints

When we fall from grace, me and you.
That's just the lies of Satan deceiving you.
That we can't be saved, but God is guiding you.
To the promised land that He'll provide for you!
If you listen closely, He'll confide in you.
His words must always reside in you.
Believe in Him, and He'll abide in you.
He gave his son, who gave his life for you.

May His grace deliver us from this grip of sin,
And free us all from this pain within.
Slaying these demons again and again
With the word of God submerged within.
This is the beginning and not the end.
But by Your side, we are destined to win.
We fight this battle as those who've sinned.
And heaven awaits us on the other end!

Pray for those who plot to deceive,
And forgive the ones who try to mislead.
Rebuke the ones who attempt to conceive
Rumors and lies for you to concede.
Resist the ones who dismiss your needs
With jealousy in mind, they ignore your deeds.
But they don't know how hard we plead,
Because all we do is pray and believe!

Our Source

I can do all things through Christ, who strengthens me.
By His stripes, we are healed and have the victory!

The war is not over, the battle rages on.
To God be the glory, but we have to be strong.

Temptation is always knocking, trying to get in.
Attempting to separate us with the glitter of sin.

We depend on God because eternal life is at stake.
Sometimes we bend, but we can never break!

He's the only one who has restored our souls.
When we were lost in the world and had no control.

No man, by themselves, will be allowed to see The Father.
Unless you believe in His Son, blood is thicker than water!

Whose name can we call on with stronger ties?
He is our strength when our faith is tried.

He is our refuge in our time of need,
He is our redeemer from the life we lead.

He is our King, not appointed by force.
And when we need to be healed, He is Our Source.

The Rebirth of My Soul

It's dark in here, somebody save me!
Where is The Father who made me?

The womb of sin has engulfed my soul.
I'm surrounded by fluids, making it hard to grab hold.

Polluted by temptation, envy, and lust.
I've been submerged in darkness for long enough.

Conceived from a grain of sand and sin's gestation.
Motivated to kick by tears of frustration.

The time has come for the world to see,
What God has created inside of me.

As I slide through the channel of the birth canal,
The light gets brighter, and I can see Him now.

The afterbirth makes me hard to hold!
But there's nothing My Doctor can't control.

As He removes the debt and sin from my flesh,
He embraces me and holds me close to His chest.

He breathes into my spirit and begins the mold.
This is the Rebirth of My Soul.

The Vine

I pray your blessings rain,
From heaven above.
Watering the seeds you plant
With heavenly love.

Saturating His roots,
With glory and praise.
And fulfilling His will,
Until the end of our days.

His love is the water
To our thirsty souls,
And His heart is the root
Of blessings untold.

His kindness and mercy
Are what we need to survive.
Witnessing His miracles,
Right in front of our eyes.

His knowledge and wisdom
Protect those in need.
From the grip of temptation,
And suffocating weeds.

WHAT IS REAL?

We've fallen from grace,
A time or two.
But we've been restored.
That's who we're connected to.

He's the Tree of Life,
And the Prince of Peace.
He's the King of saints,
That saved you and me!

If we abide in Him,
Our fruit is divine.
We are the branches,
But He is The Vine!

Reap What You Sow!

Seeds are sown on a daily basis,
In different places, to different faces.
Some will be devoured and never make it.
While others will sip from the blessed oasis.

Some will be sown on stony ground
Where the earth is shallow and barely found,
Their hopes and dreams will forever be bound
By the boulders and stones that weigh them down.

Scorched by the sun at the light of day,
The lack of a root will seal their fate.
Sometimes potential goes to waste,
Because some are destined to wither away.

Where there is no soil and no foundation,
Thorns prevent the resuscitation
Of seeds choking due to suffocation,
Because they surrendered to temptation.

In the field of righteousness, fruit will be yielded.
Serving its purpose, just as He willed it.
Satan will desperately try to steal it.
But in the presence of danger, it will be shielded.

In the right conditions, hundreds will grow.
And when the harvest is ready, we will know.
Because the faithful and righteous will begin to show,
And only then shall you Reap What You Sow!

It's All So Clear

Until I witnessed the face of Satan
standing here.
Never before,
have I seen the hand of God so clear.

He called out to me,
And said, "Child, grab on!"
My flesh was weak,
but my soul was strong.

Satan was burning down my house,
while God was opening the door.
Somebody put out this FIRE,
I can't take it anymore!

I can't even breathe –
I'm suffocating from the smoke.
When I began to choke –
I realized, this was no joke!

My roof began to collapse,
My foundation began to crack.
At that moment, I got on my knees,
and said, "Lord, please take me back."

WHAT IS REAL?

God, if you can,
please lend me Your ear.
Your intentions
have never been so clear.

Give me one more chance
to redeem my past.
The steps I have taken,
Were not on your path.

Deliver me from Satan's land,
This isn't the end of my story.
Together, You and I
will show this world Your glory.

Some will deny Your existence,
and others will cherish it dear.
Those who listen and obey
will see that it is all so clear!

His Hands

I was starving from hunger in a deserted land,
But there was no food for me because I was surrounded by sand.

Dying from a thirst that I alone could not quench,
The sand has reached places I alone could not rinse.

I've walked and crawled to the point of no return.
I pray that my journey will motivate others to learn.

My body is tired, and it is hard for me to stand.
But I know that He'll save me with the touch of His Hands.

As I was drowning, immersed in the depths of the Sea,
I witnessed His hand reaching out for me.

I was all alone, drenched in the soil of my sins.
And only He could save me from these burdens within.

My soul was submerged in the middle of the abyss.
My heart was failing, and my life was at risk.

I called on my doctor, no ordinary man.
And He saved my soul with the touch of His Hands.

Rules of the Game

The screams of the fallen call my name.
Souls are in danger of losing this game.

The board misled us and that was expected.
Learn the rules of life; challenge accepted!

Rule # 1 is to let your light shine.
Show them who you are, one play at a time!

Leave nothing to chance and move in silence.
Rule # 2 is to follow His guidance.

Nothing is more important than Rule # 3,
He said, "Worship no other god, but Me."

In this game, timeouts don't exist.
And if you time out, you will be missed.

Faith is the substance of things hoped for.
Believe in yourself! That's Rule #4.

The fifth rule of the game is for us to survive.
Because the Son of Man is still alive.

Confess with your mouth, and believe in your heart
It's rule #6 that will set us apart.

Be steadfast and unmovable, that's rule #7,
Because only the believers will make it to heaven.

When we close our eyes and walk through the gate.
To God be the glory, that's rule #8.

Follow these rules, and you'll never be the same.
Because these are the Rules of the Game.

Overcoming

One of the hardest conversations I have ever had was apologizing to my son. I wanted to tell him I was sorry for not being there when he was born. In 2005, I discovered I was the father of a four-and-a-half-year-old boy. That discovery changed my life forever. I now had to make better decisions for myself and my son. At the time, I had a steady job, but I was still battling the demons of my past. For years, I lived with constant feelings of being inadequate, misunderstood, and misjudged. I was drifting through life without any direction, too proud to seek advice, and convinced no one saw or understood the struggle I was facing. It was a constant battle, trying to achieve success but not knowing how to get there. The one thing that kept me grounded was my faith. My Christian upbringing became a lifeline, a source of strength when everything else felt uncertain.

At this point, I was in my late twenties trying to figure out what I wanted to do professionally, barely surviving financially, and learning to be a father. My life, for better or worse, was the result of the choices I had made. The only things that remained constant were my love of God and my love of writing. I spent a lot of time alone, reading, journaling, and doing the work to strengthen my relationship with Him. I knew my foundation was not strong, and if I was going to make it through, I needed to be built up from the inside out.

Over time, I had the privilege of getting to know my son better, and together we worked on building a genuine connection between us. In May 2017, I was given custody of him at a time when I found myself unemployed. After years of praying and hoping for the chance to make a significant impact on his life, that possibility became a reality. We faced challenges, and I had to mature in ways I had not before. The odds were stacked against me, but I was elated and seized this opportunity. The timing was not perfect, and I did not have much to offer financially, but I had faith and love. He had just turned sixteen that February. He was still considered a sophomore and, after changing schools three times, he was struggling. There I was, forty years old, with no stability or finances, surviving on the little savings I had and leaning heavily on God's grace. I had to be there for my son, and I was determined to show up for him and to be the father he needed. I knew God would have to play a major role in our lives if we were to survive, and I believe He did.

One of the things my son had always dreamed of doing was playing football, and I made it my mission to help make that a reality. I got him enrolled in summer school, and when football season rolled around for his junior year, he was ready to suit up. His first year of football focused on learning the game and discovering which position he wanted to play. By the time he was a senior, he knew he wanted to be a linebacker, and he had an outstanding season. He received awards for Defensive Player of the Game during both the regular season and in a playoff game. He eventually realized that I wanted nothing more than for him to achieve some of the goals he had as an adolescent. Watching him grow, succeed, and chase after his goals reminded me that all I ever wanted was for him to believe in himself—and to know that I believed in him too. I do not doubt that God was working behind the scenes through it all.

During this time, employment opportunities arose, but not the positions I could envision myself in for the long haul. Thus, I questioned where I belonged and what I was meant to do. There was always this sense that something more was out there for me—I could not quite see it yet. Eventually, my desire to be closer to God outweighed my urge to conform to society's expectations. Society had an image of me, but God has thoughts of peace, not of evil, to give us a future and hope. I began making better decisions and implementing positive changes that would impact my future outcomes.

My grandfather preached a sermon titled 'I've Got Enough,' taken from 1 Kings 19:3-4. It was about reaching the breaking point spiritually, mentally, physically, and emotionally because there were times when I was at the end of my understanding and ready to give up on life. When we are drained in one way or another, we can see nothing left for us to do but surrender. Even Elijah, one of God's prophets, felt that way—and still, God was not finished with him. I have learned that having enough is something we all go through, and we can feel like there is no hope or a way out. It is human, but when that moment comes, you have a choice. You either give up or dig deeper into your faith. No matter what I was going through, I had to stay strong and keep the faith because I had people in my life looking up to me as an example. I know that I was saved because of my faith and because I was never alone.

You Are Not Alone!

I pray your souls are saved from the torture of Satan.
because he hides in the grass, anxiously waiting.

He wants to ruin everything that we believe,
with lies and deceit, he attempts to conceive.

The burden of sin is within our flesh,
but we must understand this is only a test.

We must change our lives and the way that we live.
Determine the price and what we're willing to give.

Our spirits will guide us to the arms of Christ.
And He is ready and willing to protect your life.

No man goes to the Father except through Him.
He is the light of our lives when our paths are dim.

He's carried me through fires that have scorched my spirit,
but He never left my side, because He did not fear it.

When tribulations arise and you don't know what to do.
Take comfort in knowing that God is with you!

Believer's Peace

Harmony in chaos
That they can't understand.
Blessed by the promise of God,
And not the words of a man.

For God so loved the world,
He gave us the Prince of Peace.
And eternal life is ours
When this body is deceased.

Tribulations come
And try to weaken our faith,
But our souls are protected
By His mercy and grace.

In the midst of the storm,
Our hope could be devoured,
But our spirits are anchored
In God's all-mighty power!

Fear must not be allowed
To imprison our tranquility!
This battle will never end,
But we already have the victory!

He is our peace,
And in Him, we can rest.
He has overcome the world,
And through His blood, we are blessed.

We must reject the temptations,
And lies of the deceiver!
This battle is the price we pay
For the peace of a believer.

That's L.I.T.!

I was manipulated by a mastermind.
I never thought that life was the future of mine.
Coerced and confused beyond belief.
I was living a lie that wasn't for me.
Surrendering to a master that I never knew.
I forgot who I was, now I'm **Living In Truth.**

A lie ain't nothing for a sinner to tell,
Lessons I've learned while in the depths of hell.
I had to tell the truth and shame the devil!
I was never meant to be on his level.
As the plot got thicker, the sins did too.
I forgot who I was, now I'm **Living In Truth.**

I need His feathers to come and cover thee.
I know this is not my destiny!
I was battered and bruised with no relief.
I had to tell the truth for the world to see.
It was my shield when He rescued me.
And now I'll be L.I.T. for eternity!

The Highest Court

I've been here before.
I'm a repeat offender.
I pray for Your forgiveness,
I'm only a sinner.

If it pleases the court,
Allow me to plead my case.
The stains on my soul
Are hard to wash away.

In this testimony,
I'll provide my defense.
Hoping you understand,
Because I'm dying to repent!

During this discovery,
I present Exhibit A.
A soul born into sin
From the very first day.

Blinded by temptation
With nothing more I could see.
Constantly led astray,
This is Exhibit B.

My charges are severe,
And some I'll never forget.
For this reason alone,
I need Your Son to be my Advocate.

The prosecutor is determined
To condemn me to hell.
But I refuse to accept that sentence,
Knowing Jesus always prevails.

When we commit an offense,
This is considered a tort.
This is why I bring my case
Before The Highest Court.

Tap In

His love is unconditional,
And His promises are true!
If we believe in this,
There's something we must do.

Believe in our hearts,
And confess with our tongues,
The Lord in heaven,
Gave His only son!

He is the way,
The truth and the life!
He is the savior of a nation,
And the guiding light.

His testimony will save
The lives of men.
But one thing we must do,
We have to 'Tap-In'!

Our souls are tormented,
And stained with sin!
Dying to be free
From these burdens within.

Accept His Gift,
That belongs to us!
We are the heirs of His throne,
Conceived from dust.

Confess and repent,
That's what it requires.
Everlasting life,
That is His desire.

With His last breath,
He washed away our sins!
But one thing we must do,
We have to 'Tap-In'!

Forgive Me

I have not always been honest,
There are times I've broken my word.
Empty promises that I've spoken
When silence was preferred.

I have not always been obedient,
There are times I've gone astray.
Isolated in this place,
Surviving day by day.

I have not always been faithful,
There are times I did not serve.
Consumed with greed and rage,
I failed to put Him first.

I have not always been courageous,
There are times I've been afraid.
Feeling hopeless and abandoned
With no desire to be saved.

I have not always been innocent,
I have been guilty of sin.
I was motivated by lust,
Temptation was destined to win.

I have not always been wise,
There are times I've been a fool.
Believing I was the Alpha,
And ignoring all the rules.

I have not always been just,
There are times I've been unfair.
Leaning more to one side,
When the answer was just to share.

I have not always been saved,
Being lost is a memory.
And for that, I repent.
And I pray that God forgives me!

TRINITY

Three times denied by a close disciple.
He knew this was the test of His survival.

Three nails in His flesh, and a spear through His chest.
It was time to invest in eternal rest.

He surrendered to His accusers for the soul of man.
Because He knew this was His Father's plan.

Three puddles of blood lay under the cross,
To save the souls of those who are lost.

Three days in a tomb, secluded in a room.
Death, He consumed, so life could resume.

Saints believed that they were neglected.
But on that day, He was resurrected.

Thirty-three years He served on this earth.
Demonstrating His love and showing His worth.

Three voices will guide us, if we can hear it.
The Father, the Son, and the Holy Spirit.

Open your heart, so that you can see.
The power and glory of this TRINITY!

Precious Stone

He is the diamond in the rough
That many seek to find.
They dig for eternity,
But their soul remains blind.

Our flesh is stained,
Like coal of the earth.
And our edges are jagged
Concealing our worth.

Miners have heard
And spread rumors of Thee,
But they do not believe
What they cannot see.

Within their reach
Lies a hidden treasure,
More priceless than gold
Or desire could measure.

Unwilling to search,
Beyond their imagination.
Their souls are diluted
With vile contamination.

Seek and they shall find
A light to lead their way.
To guide them through this journey
Of darkness and dismay.

His light will show our spirit
Everything we have missed.
Protecting our souls
From all the dangers that exist.

We are children of God,
Lost and alone.
But we cannot underestimate
The power of this stone.

Heaven Cries

It was never God's intention
To watch us fail,
Because Heaven cries
When souls are condemned to hell.

Heaven sees our weakness,
We cannot hide our stains.
And when she sees us sin,
She bows her head in shame.

She's hoping and she's praying
With all of her might,
That our spirits will lead us
Through this eternal fight.

Her heart is torn
When saints concede to temptation.
She begins to weep
And prays for our salvation.

Heaven rejoices
When confessions are made,
When the lost are found,
And when souls are saved!

Her streets are gold,
And her gates are sealed.
Only chosen souls
Will see her beauty revealed.

There are so many sins
That cause her pain,
Because love is the blood
That beats in her veins.

The righteous will inherit
What the evil despise.
When we disobey God,
Heaven Cries!

Well Done!

Ye though I walk through the shadow of death,
I will praise the Lord until my last breath.
Trusting God with each and every step,
And cleansing my soul with these tears I've wept.

These demons continue to torment me,
But the spirit within carries my sword for me.
Fighting my battles and killing these beasts.
Putting my worries at ease and my soul at peace.

I've carried this cross until I could walk no more,
The weight of my sins are too heavy to ignore.
The blood of salvation is not mine, it's Yours,
And the price for glory, I am too weak to endure!

I seek wisdom and Your loving embrace.
You are my greatest fear Lord, so have Your way!
When my life comes to an end, please take me away.
"Well done," is the first thing I want to hear You say!

GRATITUDE

To the one holding this book—thank you.

Thank you for letting these poems find their way into your hands, and into your heart. Every line carries pieces of my journey, my prayers, and the quiet moments that have shaped me.

If something here made you smile, reflect, or simply feel seen—I'm grateful. That is the beauty of words. They connect us, even from afar.

I'd love to stay connected. Visit [**www.Iamthelastpoet.com**] to reach out, leave a note, or invite me to share these poems with your group or community.

With love and appreciation,

The Last Poet

www.ingramcontent.com/pod-product-compliance
Lightning Source LLC
Chambersburg PA
CBHW050919160426
43194CB00011B/2475